THE PARABLE OF THE CHEETAHS

THE PARABLE
OF THE
CHEETAHS

A Spiritual Insights Journal

DAVID A. BEDNAR

ILLUSTRATIONS BY WILSON ONG

DESERET
BOOK

Salt Lake City, Utah

Adapted from David A. Bednar, "Watchful unto Prayer Continually," *Ensign,* November 2019.

© 2020 David A. Bednar and The Boyd K. Packer Revocable Trust
Illustrations © 2020 Wilson J. Ong

DESERET BOOK is a registered trademark of Deseret Book Company.

Visit us at deseretbook.com

ISBN 978-1-62972-808-7

Printed in the United States of America
LSC Communications, Kendallville, IN

10   9   8   7   6   5   4   3   2   1

THE PARABLE OF THE CHEETAHS

DAVID A. BEDNAR

Cheetahs are the fastest land animals on earth and reach running speeds as high as 75 miles per hour. These beautiful animals can accelerate from a standstill position to running as fast as 68 miles per hour in less than three seconds.

Cheetahs are predators that sneak up on their prey
and sprint a short distance to chase and attack.

My wife, Susan, and I spent almost two hours watching two cheetahs stalking a large group of topis, Africa's most common and widespread antelopes.

The tall, dry grass of the African savanna was golden brown and almost totally obscured the predators as they pursued a group of topis. While one cheetah sat upright in the grass and did not move, the other cheetah crouched low to the ground and slowly crept closer to the unsuspecting topis.

The cheetahs were separated from each other by approximately 100 yards but worked in tandem.

Then the cheetah that had been sitting upright disappeared in the grass . . .

FIRST CHEETAH

. . . at exactly the same moment that the other cheetah sat upright.

SECOND CHEETAH

This alternating pattern of one cheetah crouching
low and creeping forward while the other cheetah sat
upright in the grass continued for a long time.

The stealthy subtlety of the strategy was intended to distract and deceive the topis and thereby divert their attention away from the approaching danger. Patiently and steadily, the two cheetahs worked as a team to secure their next meal.

Positioned between the large group of
topis and the approaching cheetahs were
several older and stronger
topis standing as sentinels on
termite mounds.

The enhanced view of the grasslands from the small hills enabled
these guardian topis to watch for signs of danger.

Then suddenly, as the cheetahs appeared
to be within striking distance, the entire
group of topis turned and ran away.

I do not know if or how the sentinel topis communicated with the larger group, but somehow a warning was given, and all the topis moved to a place of safety.

And what did the cheetahs do next? Without any delay, the two cheetahs resumed their alternating pattern of one cheetah crouching low and creeping forward while the other cheetah sat upright in the grass. The pattern of pursuit continued.

They did not stop. They did not rest or take a break. They were relentless in following their strategy of distraction and diversion.

Susan and I watched the cheetahs disappear in the distance, always moving closer and closer to the group of topis.

This experience taught many valuable lessons.

BEWARE OF EVIL'S BEGUILING DISGUISES

EXPERIENCE: Cheetahs are sleek, alluring, and captivating creatures. A cheetah's yellowish-tan to greyish-white coat with black spots acts as a beautiful disguise that makes these animals almost invisible as they stalk their prey in the African grasslands.

In a similar way, spiritually dangerous ideas and actions frequently can appear to be attractive, desirable, or pleasurable. Thus, in our contemporary world, each of us needs to be aware of beguiling bad that pretends to be good.

AS ISAIAH WARNED,

"Woe unto them that call evil good, and good evil;
that put darkness for light, and light for darkness;
that put bitter for sweet, and sweet for bitter!"

ISAIAH 5:20

WARNING: In a paradoxical period when violating the sanctity of human life is heralded as a right and chaos is described as liberty, how blessed we are to live in this latter-day dispensation when restored gospel light can shine brightly in our lives and help us to discern the adversary's dark deceptions and distractions.

"FOR THEY THAT ARE WISE AND HAVE RECEIVED THE TRUTH, AND
HAVE TAKEN THE HOLY SPIRIT FOR THEIR GUIDE, AND HAVE NOT BEEN
DECEIVED—VERILY I SAY UNTO YOU, THEY SHALL NOT BE HEWN DOWN
AND CAST INTO THE FIRE, BUT SHALL ABIDE THE DAY."

DOCTRINE AND COVENANTS 45:57

LIST SOME DECEPTIONS THE ADVERSARY TRIES TO USE AGAINST US. HOW WILL YOU RECOGNIZE AND OVERCOME THESE?

_____

_____

_____

_____

_____

_____

_____

_____

_____

_____

_____

_____

_____

_____

_____

WHEREFORE, BE NOT DECEIVED, BUT CONTINUE IN STEADFASTNESS.

DOCTRINE AND COVENANTS 49:23

STAY AWAKE AND BE ALERT

EXPERIENCE: For a topi, a brief moment of carelessness or inattentiveness could invite a swift attack from a cheetah. Likewise, spiritual complacency and casualness make us vulnerable to the advances of the adversary. Spiritual thoughtlessness invites great danger into our lives.

> Nephi described how in the latter days Satan would attempt to pacify and lull the children of God into a false sense of "carnal security, that they will say: All is well in Zion; yea, Zion prospereth, all is well—and thus the devil cheateth their souls, and leadeth them away carefully down to hell."
>
> 2 NEPHI 28:21

WARNING: Constant vigilance is required to counteract complacency and casualness. To be vigilant is the state or action of keeping careful watch for possible danger or difficulties. And keeping watch denotes the act of staying awake to guard and protect. Spiritually speaking, we need to stay awake and be alert to the promptings of the Holy Ghost and the signals that come from the Lord's watchmen on the towers.

> "YEA, AND I ALSO EXHORT YOU . . . THAT YE BE WATCHFUL UNTO PRAYER CONTINUALLY, THAT YE MAY NOT BE LED AWAY BY THE TEMPTATIONS OF THE DEVIL, . . . FOR BEHOLD, HE REWARDETH YOU NO GOOD THING."
>
> ALMA 34:39

Focusing our lives in and on the Savior and His gospel enables us to overcome the tendency of the natural man to be spiritually snoozy and lazy. As we are blessed with eyes to see and ears to hear, the Holy Ghost can increase our capacity to look and listen when we may not typically think we need to look or listen or when we may not think anything can be seen or heard.

WHAT CAN WE DO TO KEEP WATCH AND STAY SPIRITUALLY AWAKE?

WHEN HAS THE HOLY GHOST HELPED YOU DO THIS?

> **Watch, therefore, that ye may be ready.**
> DOCTRINE AND COVENANTS 50:46

UNDERSTAND THE INTENT OF THE ENEMY

EXPERIENCE: A cheetah is a predator that naturally preys on other animals. All day, every day, a cheetah is a predator.

Satan "is the enemy of righteousness and of those who seek to do the will of God" (Guide to the Scriptures, "Devil"). All day, every day, his only intent and sole purpose are to make the sons and daughters of God miserable like unto himself (see 2 Nephi 2:27).

WARNING: The Father's plan of happiness is designed to provide direction for His children, to help them experience enduring joy, and to bring them safely home to Him with resurrected, exalted bodies. The devil labors to make the sons and daughters of God confused and unhappy and to hinder their eternal progression. The adversary works relentlessly to attack the elements of the Father's plan he hates the most.

Satan does not have a body, and his eternal progress has been halted. Just as water flowing in a riverbed is stopped by a dam, so the adversary's eternal progress is thwarted because he does not have a physical body. Because of his rebellion, Lucifer has denied himself all of the mortal blessings and experiences made possible through a tabernacle of flesh and bones. One of the potent scriptural meanings of the word *damned* is illustrated in his inability to continue progressing and becoming like our Heavenly Father.

Because a physical body is so central to the Father's plan of happiness and our spiritual development, Lucifer seeks to frustrate our progression by tempting us to use our bodies improperly.

President Russell M. Nelson has taught that spiritual safety ultimately lies in "'never taking the first enticing step toward going where you should not go and doing what you should not do.' . . . As human beings we all have [physical] appetites necessary for our survival. 'These appetites are absolutely essential for the perpetuation of life. So, what does the adversary do? . . . He attacks us through our appetites. He tempts us to eat things we should not eat, to drink things we should not drink, and to love as we should not love!'"

NEWSROOM, FEB. 18, 2018

One of the ultimate ironies of eternity is that the adversary, who is miserable precisely because he has no physical body, invites and entices us to share in his misery through the improper use of our bodies. The very tool he does not have and cannot use is thus the primary target of his attempts to lure us to physical and spiritual destruction.

Understanding the intent of an enemy is vital to effective preparation for possible attacks. Precisely because Captain Moroni knew the intention of the Lamanites, he was prepared to meet them at the time of their coming and was victorious. And that same principle and promise applies to each of us.

HOW DOES SATAN TRY TO MAKE US MISERABLE ALL DAY, EVERY DAY? HOW CAN YOU PREPARE YOURSELF AGAINST HIS ATTEMPTS TO DESTROY YOU?

IF YE ARE PREPARED
YE SHALL NOT FEAR.
AND THAT YE MIGHT ESCAPE THE
POWER OF THE ENEMY.
DOCTRINE AND COVENANTS
38:30–31

AN INVITATION

Just as important lessons can be learned by observing the behavior of cheetahs and topis, so each of us should look for the lessons and warnings found in the simple events of everyday life. As we seek for a mind and heart open to receive heavenly direction by the power of the Holy Ghost, then some of the greatest instructions that we can receive and many of the most powerful warnings that can safeguard us will originate in our own ordinary experiences. Powerful parables are contained in both the scriptures and in our daily lives.

I have highlighted only three of the many lessons that can be identified in the adventure Susan and I had in Africa. I invite and encourage you to reflect on this episode with the cheetahs and the topis and identify additional lessons for you and your family. Please remember always that your home is the true center of gospel learning and living.

A PROMISE

As you respond in faith to this invitation, inspired thoughts will come to your mind, spiritual feelings will swell in your heart, and you will recognize actions that should be undertaken or continued so that you can "take upon you [the] whole armor [of God], that ye may be able to withstand the evil day, having done all, that ye may be able to stand."

DOCTRINE AND COVENANTS 27:15

I promise that the blessings of effective preparation and spiritual protection will flow into your life as you are watchful unto prayer vigilantly and continually.

AN APOSTLE'S TESTIMONY

I testify that pressing forward on the covenant path provides spiritual safety and invites enduring joy into our lives. And I witness that the risen and living Savior will sustain and strengthen us in times both good and bad.

DAVID A. BEDNAR

OUR
SPIRITUAL INSIGHTS
JOURNAL

Suggestions for using this journal:

- Be watchful for observations and experiences that could relate to powerful spiritual lessons. Encourage members of your family or friends to do the same.

- At dinnertime, during family home evening, in family councils, or with your friends, discuss additional lessons found in the cheetah story and new lessons discovered from scripture study or everyday life experiences.

- Invite a family member or friend to share a life experience and a lesson found through that experience. Others might offer additional insights they may have seen in the experience.

- Search for scriptures or counsel from Church leaders related to the lesson or gospel principle.

- Record a short name for the lesson, the experience and the gospel principle it teaches, related scriptures or counsel, the lesson or warning, actions you decide are appropriate to take based on what you have learned, and blessings discovered as a result of taking action.

Lesson:

....

DATE:

_____

EXPERIENCE:

_____

_____

_____

_____

SCRIPTURE OR COUNSEL FROM CHURCH LEADERS:

_____

_____

_____

_____

LESSON OR WARNING:

_____

_____

_____

_____

ACTIONS TO TAKE:

_____

_____

_____

_____

BLESSINGS DISCOVERED:

_____

_____

_____

Lesson:

DATE:

EXPERIENCE:

SCRIPTURE OR COUNSEL FROM CHURCH LEADERS:

LESSON OR WARNING:

ACTIONS TO TAKE:

BLESSINGS DISCOVERED:

Lesson:

DATE:

EXPERIENCE:

SCRIPTURE OR COUNSEL FROM CHURCH LEADERS:

LESSON OR WARNING:

ACTIONS TO TAKE:

BLESSINGS DISCOVERED:

Lesson:

DATE:

EXPERIENCE:

SCRIPTURE OR COUNSEL FROM CHURCH LEADERS:

LESSON OR WARNING:

ACTIONS TO TAKE:

BLESSINGS DISCOVERED:

Lesson:

....

DATE:

_____

EXPERIENCE:

_____

_____

_____

_____

SCRIPTURE OR COUNSEL FROM CHURCH LEADERS:

_____

_____

_____

LESSON OR WARNING:

_____

_____

_____

_____

ACTIONS TO TAKE:

_____

_____

_____

_____

BLESSINGS DISCOVERED:

_____

_____

_____

_____

Lesson:

DATE:

EXPERIENCE:

SCRIPTURE OR COUNSEL FROM CHURCH LEADERS:

LESSON OR WARNING:

ACTIONS TO TAKE:

BLESSINGS DISCOVERED:

Lesson:

DATE:

EXPERIENCE:

SCRIPTURE OR COUNSEL FROM CHURCH LEADERS:

LESSON OR WARNING:

ACTIONS TO TAKE:

BLESSINGS DISCOVERED:

Lesson:

DATE:

EXPERIENCE:

SCRIPTURE OR COUNSEL FROM CHURCH LEADERS:

LESSON OR WARNING:

ACTIONS TO TAKE:

BLESSINGS DISCOVERED:

Lesson:

DATE:

EXPERIENCE:

SCRIPTURE OR COUNSEL FROM CHURCH LEADERS:

LESSON OR WARNING:

ACTIONS TO TAKE:

BLESSINGS DISCOVERED:

Lesson:

....

DATE:

EXPERIENCE:

SCRIPTURE OR COUNSEL FROM CHURCH LEADERS:

LESSON OR WARNING:

ACTIONS TO TAKE:

BLESSINGS DISCOVERED:

Lesson:

DATE:

EXPERIENCE:

SCRIPTURE OR COUNSEL FROM CHURCH LEADERS:

LESSON OR WARNING:

ACTIONS TO TAKE:

BLESSINGS DISCOVERED:

Lesson:

DATE:

EXPERIENCE:

SCRIPTURE OR COUNSEL FROM CHURCH LEADERS:

LESSON OR WARNING:

ACTIONS TO TAKE:

BLESSINGS DISCOVERED:

Lesson:

DATE:

EXPERIENCE:

SCRIPTURE OR COUNSEL FROM CHURCH LEADERS:

LESSON OR WARNING:

ACTIONS TO TAKE:

BLESSINGS DISCOVERED:

Lesson:

....

DATE:

_____

EXPERIENCE:

_____
_____
_____
_____

SCRIPTURE OR COUNSEL FROM CHURCH LEADERS:

_____
_____
_____
_____

LESSON OR WARNING:

_____
_____
_____
_____

ACTIONS TO TAKE:

_____
_____
_____
_____

BLESSINGS DISCOVERED:

_____
_____
_____
_____

Lesson:

....

DATE:
_____

EXPERIENCE:
_____
_____
_____
_____

SCRIPTURE OR COUNSEL FROM CHURCH LEADERS:
_____
_____
_____
_____

LESSON OR WARNING:
_____
_____
_____
_____

ACTIONS TO TAKE:
_____
_____
_____
_____

BLESSINGS DISCOVERED:
_____
_____
_____
_____

Lesson:

....

DATE:

_____

EXPERIENCE:

_____
_____
_____
_____

SCRIPTURE OR COUNSEL FROM CHURCH LEADERS:

_____
_____
_____
_____

LESSON OR WARNING:

_____
_____
_____
_____

ACTIONS TO TAKE:

_____
_____
_____
_____

BLESSINGS DISCOVERED:

_____
_____
_____
_____

Lesson:

DATE:

EXPERIENCE:

SCRIPTURE OR COUNSEL FROM CHURCH LEADERS:

LESSON OR WARNING:

ACTIONS TO TAKE:

BLESSINGS DISCOVERED:

Lesson:

DATE:

EXPERIENCE:

SCRIPTURE OR COUNSEL FROM CHURCH LEADERS:

LESSON OR WARNING:

ACTIONS TO TAKE:

BLESSINGS DISCOVERED:

Lesson:

....

DATE:

_____

EXPERIENCE:

_____
_____
_____
_____

SCRIPTURE OR COUNSEL FROM CHURCH LEADERS:

_____
_____
_____

LESSON OR WARNING:

_____
_____
_____
_____

ACTIONS TO TAKE:

_____
_____
_____

BLESSINGS DISCOVERED:

_____
_____
_____
_____

Lesson:

....

DATE:

EXPERIENCE:

SCRIPTURE OR COUNSEL FROM CHURCH LEADERS:

LESSON OR WARNING:

ACTIONS TO TAKE:

BLESSINGS DISCOVERED:

Lesson:

....

DATE:

_____

EXPERIENCE:

_____

_____

_____

_____

SCRIPTURE OR COUNSEL FROM CHURCH LEADERS:

_____

_____

_____

_____

LESSON OR WARNING:

_____

_____

_____

_____

ACTIONS TO TAKE:

_____

_____

_____

_____

BLESSINGS DISCOVERED:

_____

_____

_____

_____

Lesson:

DATE:

EXPERIENCE:

SCRIPTURE OR COUNSEL FROM CHURCH LEADERS:

LESSON OR WARNING:

ACTIONS TO TAKE:

BLESSINGS DISCOVERED:

Lesson:

DATE:

EXPERIENCE:

SCRIPTURE OR COUNSEL FROM CHURCH LEADERS:

LESSON OR WARNING:

ACTIONS TO TAKE:

BLESSINGS DISCOVERED:

THE PARABLE OF THE CROCODILES

THE PARABLE
OF THE
CROCODILES

A Spiritual Insights Journal

BOYD K. PACKER

ILLUSTRATIONS BY WILSON ONG

DESERET
BOOK

Salt Lake City, Utah

Adapted from Boyd K. Packer, "Spiritual Crocodiles," *Ensign,* May 1976.

© 2020 David A. Bednar and The Boyd K. Packer Revocable Trust
Illustrations © 2020 Wilson J. Ong

Visit us at deseretbook.com

ISBN 978-1-62972-808-7

Printed in the United States of America
LSC Communications, Kendallville, IN

10   9   8   7   6   5   4   3   2   1

THE PARABLE
OF THE CROCODILES

—⦿—

BOYD K. PACKER

I have always been interested in animals and birds and when I was a little boy and the other children wanted to play cowboy, I wanted to go on safari to Africa.

When I learned to read, I found books about birds and animals and came to know much about them. By the time I was in my teens I could identify most of the African animals. I could tell a klipspringer from an impala, or a gemsbok from wildebeest.

Klipspringer

Impala

Wildebeest

Gemsbok

I always wanted to go to Africa and see the animals, and finally that opportunity came. Sister Packer and I were assigned to tour the South Africa Mission.

We had a very strenuous schedule and had
dedicated eight chapels in seven days, scattered
across that broad continent.

The mission president was vague about the schedule for September 10th. (That happens to be my birthday.) We were in Rhodesia, planning, I thought, to return to Johannesburg, South Africa. But he had other plans, and we landed at Victoria Falls.

"There is a game reserve some distance from here, and I have rented a car, and tomorrow, your birthday, we are going to spend seeing the African animals."

The next day, a young ranger drove us to a lookout over a water hole. On the way to the lookout he volunteered to show us some lions. He turned off through the brush and before long located a group of seventeen lions all sprawled out asleep and drove right up among them.

We stopped at a water hole to watch the animals come to drink. It was very dry that season and there was not much water, really just muddy spots. When the elephants stepped into the soft mud the water would seep into the depression and the animals would drink from the elephant tracks.

The antelope, particularly, were very nervous. They would approach the mud hole, only to turn and run away in great fright. I could see there were no lions about and asked the guide why they didn't drink.

His answer, and this is the lesson, was

"CROCODILES."

I knew he must be joking and asked him seriously,

"WHAT IS THE PROBLEM?"

The answer again:

"CROCODILES."

"NONSENSE. THERE ARE NO CROCODILES OUT THERE. ANYONE CAN SEE THAT."

I thought he was having some fun at the expense of his foreign game expert, and finally I asked him to tell us the truth. Now I remind you that I was not uninformed. I had read many books. Besides, anyone would know that you can't hide a crocodile in an elephant track.

He could tell I did not believe him and determined, I suppose, to teach me a lesson. We drove to another location where the car was on an embankment above the muddy hole where we could look down. "There. See for yourself."

I couldn't see anything except the mud, a little water, and the nervous animals in the distance. Then all at once I saw it!—a large crocodile, settled in the mud, waiting for some unsuspecting animal to get thirsty enough to come for a drink.

Suddenly I became a believer! When he could see I was willing to listen, he continued with the lesson.

"THERE ARE CROCODILES ALL OVER THE PARK, NOT JUST IN THE RIVERS. WE DON'T HAVE ANY WATER WITHOUT A CROCODILE SOMEWHERE NEAR IT, AND YOU'D BETTER COUNT ON IT."

The guide was kinder to me than I deserved. My "know-it-all" challenge to his first statement, "crocodiles," might have brought an invitation, "Well, go out and see for yourself!"

I could see for myself that there were no crocodiles. I was so sure of myself I think I might have walked out just to see what was there. Such an arrogant approach could have been fatal! But he was patient enough to teach me.

I hope you'll be wiser in talking to your guides than I was on that occasion. That smart-aleck idea that I knew everything really wasn't worthy of me, nor is it worthy of you. I'm not very proud of it, and I think I'd be ashamed to tell you about it except that telling you may help you.

LISTEN TO YOUR GUIDES

EXPERIENCE: Those ahead of you in life have probed about the water holes a bit and raise a voice of warning about crocodiles. Not just the big, gray lizards that can bite you to pieces, but spiritual crocodiles, infinitely more dangerous, and more deceptive and less visible, even, than those well-camouflaged reptiles of Africa.

These spiritual crocodiles can kill or mutilate your souls. They can destroy your peace of mind and the peace of mind of those who love you. Those are the ones to be warned against, and there is hardly a watering place in all of mortality now that is not infested with them.

WARNING: Fortunately there are guides enough in life to prevent these things from happening if we are willing to take counsel now and again.

Some of us are appointed now, as you will be soon, to be guides and rangers. Now we don't use those titles very much. We go under the titles of parents—father and mother—bishop, leader, adviser. Our assignment is to see that you get through mortality without being injured by these spiritual crocodiles.

WHAT OR WHERE ARE SOME OF THE SPIRITUAL CROCODILES THAT LIE IN WAIT IN YOUR LIFE? WHO ARE THE GUIDES IN YOUR LIFE? WHAT CAN YOU DO TO MORE FULLY TRUST, FOLLOW, AND SUPPORT THEM?

LEARN HOW TO RECEIVE REVELATION

EXPERIENCE: All of the training and activity in the Church has as its central purpose a desire to see you free and independent and secure, both spiritually and temporally.

If you will listen to the counsel of your parents and your teachers and your leaders when you are young, you can learn how to follow the best guide of all—the whisperings of the Holy Spirit. That is individual revelation. There is a process through which we can be alerted to spiritual dangers. Just as surely as that guide warned me, you can receive signals alerting you to the spiritual crocodiles that lurk ahead.

WARNING: If we can train you to listen to these spiritual communications, you will be protected from these crocodiles of life. You can learn what it feels like to be guided from on high. This inspiration can come to you now, in all of your activities, in school, and dating—not just in your Church assignments.

LEARN HOW TO PRAY AND HOW TO RECEIVE ANSWERS TO YOUR PRAYERS. WHEN YOU PRAY OVER SOME THINGS, YOU MUST PATIENTLY WAIT A LONG, LONG TIME BEFORE YOU WILL RECEIVE AN ANSWER. SOME PRAYERS, FOR YOUR OWN SAFETY, MUST BE ANSWERED IMMEDIATELY, AND SOME PROMPTINGS WILL EVEN COME WHEN YOU HAVEN'T PRAYED AT ALL.

WHAT ACTIONS CAN YOU TAKE TO SEEK AND RECEIVE PERSONAL REVELATION? HOW CAN YOU RECOGNIZE THE GUIDANCE OF THE HOLY GHOST? WHAT EVIDENCES HAVE YOU SEEN THAT PRAYERS HAVE BEEN ANSWERED?

AN INVITATION

Once you really determine to follow that guide, your testimony will grow and you will find provisions set out along the way in unexpected places, as evidence that someone knew that you would be traveling that way.

The basic exercise for you to perform to become spiritually strong and to become independent lies in obedience to your guides. If you will follow them and do it willingly, you can learn to trust those delicate, sensitive, spiritual promptings. You will learn that they always, invariably, lead you to do that which is righteous.

A PROMISE

I have learned from experience the meaning of the scripture:

> "If ye continue in my word,
> then are ye my disciples indeed;
> And ye shall know the truth, and
> the truth shall make you free."

JOHN 8:31–32

I have been nipped a time or two and on occasion have needed some spiritual first aid, but have been otherwise saved because I have been warned.

Fortunately, there is spiritual first aid for those who have been bitten. The bishop of the ward is the guide in charge of this first aid. He can also treat those who have been badly morally mauled by these spiritual crocodiles—and see them completely healed.

AN APOSTLE'S
TESTIMONY

That experience in Africa was another reminder for me to follow the Guide. I follow Him because I want to. I bear witness that He lives, that Jesus is the Christ. I know that He has a body of flesh and bones, that He directs this Church, and His purpose is to see all of us guided safely back into His presence.

BOYD K. PACKER

OUR SPIRITUAL INSIGHTS JOURNAL

Suggestions for using this journal:

- Be watchful for observations and experiences that could relate to powerful spiritual lessons. Encourage members of your family or friends to do the same.

- At dinnertime, during family home evening, in family councils, or with your friends, discuss additional lessons found in the crocodile story and new lessons discovered from scripture study or everyday life experiences.

- Invite a family member or friend to share a life experience and a lesson found through that experience. Others might offer additional insights they may have seen in the experience.

- Search for scriptures or counsel from Church leaders related to the lesson or gospel principle.

- Record a short name for the lesson, the experience and the gospel principle it teaches, related scriptures or counsel, the lesson or warning, actions you decide are appropriate to take based on what you have learned, and blessings discovered as a result of taking action.

Lesson:

....

DATE:

_____

EXPERIENCE:

_____
_____
_____
_____

SCRIPTURE OR COUNSEL FROM CHURCH LEADERS:

_____
_____
_____

LESSON OR WARNING:

_____
_____
_____

ACTIONS TO TAKE:

_____
_____
_____

BLESSINGS DISCOVERED:

_____
_____
_____

Lesson:

DATE:

EXPERIENCE:

SCRIPTURE OR COUNSEL FROM CHURCH LEADERS:

LESSON OR WARNING:

ACTIONS TO TAKE:

BLESSINGS DISCOVERED:

Lesson:

....

DATE:

EXPERIENCE:

SCRIPTURE OR COUNSEL FROM CHURCH LEADERS:

LESSON OR WARNING:

ACTIONS TO TAKE:

BLESSINGS DISCOVERED:

Lesson:

....

DATE:

EXPERIENCE:

SCRIPTURE OR COUNSEL FROM CHURCH LEADERS:

LESSON OR WARNING:

ACTIONS TO TAKE:

BLESSINGS DISCOVERED:

Lesson:

....

DATE:

_____

EXPERIENCE:

_____
_____
_____
_____

SCRIPTURE OR COUNSEL FROM CHURCH LEADERS:

_____
_____
_____
_____

LESSON OR WARNING:

_____
_____
_____
_____

ACTIONS TO TAKE:

_____
_____
_____
_____

BLESSINGS DISCOVERED:

_____
_____
_____

Lesson:

DATE:

EXPERIENCE:

SCRIPTURE OR COUNSEL FROM CHURCH LEADERS:

LESSON OR WARNING:

ACTIONS TO TAKE:

BLESSINGS DISCOVERED:

Lesson:

....

DATE:

EXPERIENCE:

SCRIPTURE OR COUNSEL FROM CHURCH LEADERS:

LESSON OR WARNING:

ACTIONS TO TAKE:

BLESSINGS DISCOVERED:

Lesson:

DATE:

EXPERIENCE:

SCRIPTURE OR COUNSEL FROM CHURCH LEADERS:

LESSON OR WARNING:

ACTIONS TO TAKE:

BLESSINGS DISCOVERED:

Lesson:

....

DATE:

EXPERIENCE:

SCRIPTURE OR COUNSEL FROM CHURCH LEADERS:

LESSON OR WARNING:

ACTIONS TO TAKE:

BLESSINGS DISCOVERED:

Lesson:

....

DATE:

_____

EXPERIENCE:

_____

_____

_____

_____

SCRIPTURE OR COUNSEL FROM CHURCH LEADERS:

_____

_____

_____

_____

LESSON OR WARNING:

_____

_____

_____

_____

ACTIONS TO TAKE:

_____

_____

_____

_____

BLESSINGS DISCOVERED:

_____

_____

_____

_____

Lesson:

DATE:

EXPERIENCE:

SCRIPTURE OR COUNSEL FROM CHURCH LEADERS:

LESSON OR WARNING:

ACTIONS TO TAKE:

BLESSINGS DISCOVERED:

Lesson:

DATE:

EXPERIENCE:

SCRIPTURE OR COUNSEL FROM CHURCH LEADERS:

LESSON OR WARNING:

ACTIONS TO TAKE:

BLESSINGS DISCOVERED:

Lesson:

DATE:

EXPERIENCE:

SCRIPTURE OR COUNSEL FROM CHURCH LEADERS:

LESSON OR WARNING:

ACTIONS TO TAKE:

BLESSINGS DISCOVERED:

Lesson:

DATE:

EXPERIENCE:

SCRIPTURE OR COUNSEL FROM CHURCH LEADERS:

LESSON OR WARNING:

ACTIONS TO TAKE:

BLESSINGS DISCOVERED:

Lesson:

DATE:

EXPERIENCE:

SCRIPTURE OR COUNSEL FROM CHURCH LEADERS:

LESSON OR WARNING:

ACTIONS TO TAKE:

BLESSINGS DISCOVERED:

Lesson:

....

DATE:

EXPERIENCE:

SCRIPTURE OR COUNSEL FROM CHURCH LEADERS:

LESSON OR WARNING:

ACTIONS TO TAKE:

BLESSINGS DISCOVERED:

Lesson:

....

DATE:

EXPERIENCE:

SCRIPTURE OR COUNSEL FROM CHURCH LEADERS:

LESSON OR WARNING:

ACTIONS TO TAKE:

BLESSINGS DISCOVERED:

Lesson:

....

DATE:

_____

EXPERIENCE:

_____
_____
_____
_____

SCRIPTURE OR COUNSEL FROM CHURCH LEADERS:

_____
_____
_____
_____

LESSON OR WARNING:

_____
_____
_____
_____

ACTIONS TO TAKE:

_____
_____
_____
_____

BLESSINGS DISCOVERED:

_____
_____
_____
_____

Lesson:

....

DATE:

_____

EXPERIENCE:

_____
_____
_____
_____

SCRIPTURE OR COUNSEL FROM CHURCH LEADERS:

_____
_____
_____

LESSON OR WARNING:

_____
_____
_____

ACTIONS TO TAKE:

_____
_____
_____

BLESSINGS DISCOVERED:

_____
_____
_____

Lesson:

DATE:

EXPERIENCE:

SCRIPTURE OR COUNSEL FROM CHURCH LEADERS:

LESSON OR WARNING:

ACTIONS TO TAKE:

BLESSINGS DISCOVERED:

Lesson:

....

DATE:

_____

EXPERIENCE:

_____
_____
_____
_____

SCRIPTURE OR COUNSEL FROM CHURCH LEADERS:

_____
_____
_____

LESSON OR WARNING:

_____
_____
_____

ACTIONS TO TAKE:

_____
_____
_____

BLESSINGS DISCOVERED:

_____
_____
_____

Lesson:

....

DATE:

EXPERIENCE:

SCRIPTURE OR COUNSEL FROM CHURCH LEADERS:

LESSON OR WARNING:

ACTIONS TO TAKE:

BLESSINGS DISCOVERED:

Lesson:

DATE:

EXPERIENCE:

SCRIPTURE OR COUNSEL FROM CHURCH LEADERS:

LESSON OR WARNING:

ACTIONS TO TAKE:

BLESSINGS DISCOVERED: